T0146963

Situational Praise

PATRICIA YARBROUGH

authorHOUSE®

AuthorHouse™
1663 Liberty Drive
Bloomington, IN 47403
www.authorhouse.com
Phone: 1 (800) 839-8640

© 2019 Patricia Yarbrough. All rights reserved.

No part of this book may be reproduced, stored in a retrieval system, or transmitted by any means without the written permission of the author.

Published by AuthorHouse 09/27/2019

ISBN: 978-1-7283-2931-4 (sc)
ISBN: 978-1-7283-2929-1 (hc)
ISBN: 978-1-7283-2930-7 (e)

Library of Congress Control Number: 2019915274

Print information available on the last page.

Any people depicted in stock imagery provided by Getty Images are models, and such images are being used for illustrative purposes only. Certain stock imagery © Getty Images.

This book is printed on acid-free paper.

Because of the dynamic nature of the Internet, any web addresses or links contained in this book may have changed since publication and may no longer be valid. The views expressed in this work are solely those of the author and do not necessarily reflect the views of the publisher, and the publisher hereby disclaims any responsibility for them.

CONTENTS

THE PURPOSE FOR WRITING A BOOK OF POETRY AND SONG LYRICS

The reason for writing this book of poetry is to offer words of encouragement to individuals who are going through different situations in their live and need a ray of hope. I also wrote various poems for people who would like to express gratitude to others, but cannot direct what they feel in words. My poems will offer illustration of thoughts for someone to use. Future aspirations is to put my poems in plagues form so someone can purchase them to give for a momentum of their appreciation of others.

LOVE YOURSELF

You have to learn to love yourself
Because if you don't love you why look for someone else
You have to love what you see
Be kind to yourself and don't be mean
We have red heads, blondes, black heads and brunettes
We have brown skin, blue black, white, and yellow
Don't be ashamed of yourself just be mellow
You have to appreciate yourself and love who you are
Achieve your dreams and conquer your fears in life
Remember in this world there is misery and strife
Strive to be what God want you to be
For the love of Christ will set you free
Remember to never look down but always ahead
Live your life and do not act like your dead
You have to learn to love yourself before you can love anyone else

LOVE, THE SINGLE MAN

Single man will where I find you today
Do you have a job or do you just play
Are you strong, self-sufficient, and supply your own needs
Do you have a sugar momma giving you to please
A woman loves a man who is strong
A man with a good head on his shoulder and know what he wants
You do not have to drive the finest car
Wear name brand clothes or have a million-dollar job
Just be a good provider and show her some love
Single man it's ok if you want to enjoy your life
And wait to hook up with someone else
Enjoy your freedom, enjoy your time alone
Until you want to share your life
And give a home to the woman you call your wife

LOVE, THE SINGLE WOMAN

The single woman sometimes desires to have to have a man
But she is waiting on God she can withstand
She is self-sufficient and she rely on herself
She considers being single a blessing and not a curse
Sure she may want to get married one day
But if God doesn't bless her with one she will remain single unto the grave
See living single is not bad at all
Because you give up your freedom, you are bound for life
So single women don't feel bad at all
You can go when you want come when you please
You can cook when you want to or eat out when you can
You don't have to answer to a man
Single woman you need to make sure you are satisfied with yourself
Before you try to hook up with someone else
Look around you and enjoy who you are
Don't let no one put you down, abuse, or misuse you
You are a beautiful woman
Keep your head uplifted to the sky
Life have no limits, go ahead girl and fly high
Remember living single is a blessing and not a curse
Read your Bible and find you a verse

UNCONDITIONAL LOVE

Unconditional love
Is loving someone who do not love you
Is caring for someone who do not care for themselves
Unconditional love
Is loving someone despite the circumstances
Is able to overlook faults to see the need
Unconditional love
Is what God gives to man kind
When He gave His son up for us to die
Unconditional love
Is loving someone who rejects you
Unconditional love
Is the love God have for people
Yet, a man will not accept God's unconditional love

COME BACK MY LOVE

I loved you with you with an everlasting love
I talked to you with a still small voice
I did not force myself on you but I gave you a choice
To dine with me forever and others to forsake
But instead you chose to leave me and I let you escape
Why did you turn away, when I held my arms out to you
I was your shield, your buckler, your healer, your friend
No one on earth can treat you like I can
Come back my love, return to me
I am the only one who can set you free
Come back my love let me love you today, for tomorrow may be too late
Come back my love, while it's drawing time
For soon I will say, so long and good bye

JUST A PIECE OF DIRT

I'm just a piece of dirt
How shall I be afraid when God has my life
I will remember what He said in His Word and commit myself to Him.

ONE SIDED LOVER

With a one sided lover romance will not last
Because she is too busy looking in a one- way glass
She wants everything her way or nothing at all
She desires her man to jump as soon as she call
She never fixes him breakfast, lunch, or dinner too
He has to order take out or fix his own meals
One sided lover how long you think your love will last
You're driving your man to another woman's path
He tried to listen to you and to him you turn a death ear
He is going to leave you and find someone who cares
How long do you imagine your beauty will last
You need to start showing your husband love
Before he finds himself a new wife
One sided lover love comes two ways
You need to wake up before you start to see lonely days
God help the woman who only love one way
Let her realize it takes both of them to play

SIGNS OF LOVE

The glare in the eye
The smile on the face
Is a sign of love come your way
The panting of your heart as he walk your way
His presence brighten up your day
The smell of his aroma lingers in the air
Embraces you as the thought of him echoes in your mind
The signs of love has come, hopefully he will say you are the one
Maybe he will ask you to be his bride
Or will he duck and hide
Is a sign of love come your way
This is the time you need to pray
Make sure he is the right one for you
So in the future you will not be sad and blue
If a sign of love come your way
Take it slow and do not haste
The sign of love can be special and sweet
Especially if you love the one you meet
Is this your time of love

Family

A MOTHERLESS MOTHER

I was birthed by my mother, but let me lye alone
She was not there to hear me cry or moan
I could see her far away, someone else she directed to my path
My heart was too broken to laugh
O mom why did you bear, me
I wish you have given me away
To a family who would have cherish me
Instead of you who go astray
No nurturing from you I received
Now I must in my heart grieve
Mourn for the children who have mothers who do not care
I pray their cry God will hear
The broken hearts the Lord will heal
And God will shine a light through their lives
So they will know they do not need to live in misery and strife
But they will know in Christ they shall have eternal life

MOM I THANK GOD FOR YOU

Mom, you encourage me to dream
You encourage me to be what God want me to be
How can I repay you for all the things that you do
I thank God for you
Mom, you're the one who cheered me up when I was down
You know how to put a smile on my face when you see a frown
I thank God for you
Mom, when your schedule was busy you manage to find time with me
    to spend
I thank God for you
Mom you are so special
One day I want to be like you
Inspiring others to be like God and telling them there able to go through
I thank God for you

MOTHER FIGURE

Some children are raised by parents
Some by aunts, uncles, grandparents, and friends
Some children are raised by the streets and strangers
Some children have people come into their life
Who takes them in and love them like their family
And treat them like they are one of their own
She covers them like a mother hen and with her wings she takes them in
She's a mother that never gave birth
Thou her womb remain close
She nurtures her young
She instills hope and love into their being
To them she is the only mother they know
She is the one they will cherish in their heart
For to them she was like a mother
For she is their mother figure

MOTHER

I have a mother who is there for me
There was a time she would bounce me on her knees
Now, I am no longer a child
I am all grown up
For mother now, for you I should fuss
I should make sure she is eating well
Clean her house or wash a dish or two
For I shall tell you mother, I am here for you
To do the things you need me to do
Now that the role has change
I can say the feelings feel strange
But one thing I shall never forget
Is my mother's love

MOTHER (2)

Mother, the sun shines as you enter the room
You have the personality of a blossoming flower
As you walk you separate the rivers that are in your path
Your wisdom enlightens my worries
Mother how I behold your beauty as days go by
As the wrinkles appear and gray hairs begin to show
I am glad to be called your child
To have the pleasure to sit at your feet
And listen to the stories you have to tell
Mother you shall always be precious to me
For you shall be a treasure I cherish for the rest of my days

MOTHER ROLE CHANGE

I have a mother who is there for me
There was a time she used to bounce me on her knees
Now, I am no longer a child, I am all grown up
For mother, now, I should fuss
I should make sure she is eating well
And all her needs are met
I should give her a helping hand
Clean her house or wash a dish or two
For I shall tell mother, I am here for you
To do the things you need me to do
Now that the roles have change
I can say the feelings feel strange
But one thing I shall never forget is a mother's love

MOTHER

Mother, the sun shines as you enter the room
You have the personality of a blossoming flower
As you walk you separate the rivers that are in your path
Your wisdom enlightens my worries
Mother how I behold your beauty as days go by
As the wrinkles a appear and gray hairs begin to show
I am glad to be called your child
To have the pleasure to sit at your feet
And listen to the stories you have to tell
Mother, you shall always be precious to me
For you shall be a treasure I cherish for the rest of my days

BE LIKE MY MOTHER (2)

As I look in the mirror
I see I resemble you
If it wasn't for you mother, I do not know what to do
Your beauty is not only outward, but inwardly too
As I go in prayer, I always thank God for you
A mothers' love goes beyond situations and circumstances too
They know how to go to God
They say Lord protect my child and give them what they need
For a mother's love is so sweet
Oh mother all I can say
I thank God for you everyday
For all the sacrifices you made for me
For you are one of God's precious being

A FATHER TO THE FATHERLESS

There are children growing up without a father in the home
Left alone to roam the streets to roam
Sometimes boys feel insecure and little girls too
Because they do not have a man at home to look up to
But we do not have no reason to fear because God is always near
He will love us always and for you He will be the father you need
He said He will be a father to the fatherless
The Lord will be your protector, shield you from danger
He will be your provider God will make sure your needs are met
God will be your Comforter
He will comfort you when you need peace
All you have to do is acknowledge the Lord as your Savior and friend
He will stick with you through the good times and bad
God will take your sadness and make you glad
That you let Him in your life
Your heavenly Father cares for you and want to be in your life continually

FATHER

Father the man I looked for to be the head of my house
Father, the man who took my mother to be his wife
Father, the one who provided for my needs
Father the one who walked me to the park and played games with me.
Father, the one who inspired me to take my manly characteristics
And taught my sister what to look for in a man
Father as days go by and you age show
I want you to know how I love you so
For being a wonderful man
I hope to walk in your footsteps
And be a father to my children as you were for me
And may your legacy continue from generation to generation
For you to me is the greatest father in the nation

THE FATHER I LOVE

You did not wear the name brand clothes
Or drive the fineness car
But a true good father you are to me
You taught me how to respect my elders
You taught me how to appreciate life, more than the pleasures of the land
You taught me to work for the things I desire
Not to live from handouts of other men
You taught me how to be thankful for the small things in life
Father how can I thank you
For the good strong character, you hold
It did not matter what others thought of you
Because you knew you were a man and you knew what you had to do
You are a protector to my mother
You taught my sisters what they should expect from a man
I thank God for giving me a man like you
You are the king of your castle and you rule well
Father I just want to say I love you

THE FATHER THAT WAS NOT THERE

Dad where were you when I needed to learn how to tie my shoes
Dad where were you when I needed a father to look up to
Dad where were you when mommy had to work day and night
Just so the rent she could pay
I waited to see if you would come around
I longed for your presence, but you I did not see
I wonder if you even care for me
I was left with emptiness inside
Because I did not have my father as a guide
I am sorry you did not see me grow up to be a man
Because you are the father that was not there

FATHER THANK YOU

God our Heavenly Father sacrificed His only, Son, to free mankind
   from sin.
That was the greatest love shown to men.
As our heavenly father hold us in the palm of His hands.
Dad, I can remember when you bounce me on your knees.
And as God provided for us, you provided for me.
I never had to beg or sell drugs on the streets.
You are the kind of father every son truly needs
I can remember hearing you at night praying for me.
Father how I miss holding your hand and hear you telling me I can
Father I thank God for the testimony of your life
Father you are a hero to me
I shall hold on to your advice and make sure I keep Christ in my life

BROTHER TO BROTHER

Brother, I was the quiet one
You were the popular one
I had less friends
You were friends with everyone
Although we were different in many ways
No one could take our brotherly love away
We did all the things brother do
After we grew up we moved away
You went one direction and I went the other way
But when we come together we reconnect
No love was lost, thou less time we spent
We are brothers and we love one another
This relationship we share with no one
This is brother to brother

BROTHER DONT YOU CRY

Brother don't you cry because things do not go your way
Just pick up the pieces and begin to pray
Brother don't you cry, because you lost your job
Just keep on looking until you get another boss
Brother don't you cry
It is not time to give up
Even thou life has thrown a couple of bad punches
It is not time to keep fussing
You have to keep working hard to follow your dreams
Even thou you feel like throwing up your arms and scream
Life is made with many challenges and you cannot never give up
Brother don't you cry, just keep the faith
And live life day by day

BROTHER

My big brother is special to me
Brother, another male in the family
Sisters look up to him
Little brothers like to be like him
Brother, growing up to be a man
I hope you conquer your dreams and be all you can be
Brother, take care of your responsibilities
Do not spend your time hanging in the streets
Brother you will always be my friend even thou we are kin
Brother carry on the family name
Live respectfully not in shame

LIKE A SISTER

We went to school together
We were the closest of friends
We told each other secrets
With others we did not share
We dress alike all the time others would call us twins
Even though we share no blood
Our love was thicker than water
Now, that we are grown up and we only call from time to time
Our love for each other still in twines
I am glad I have a friend I can lean on and talk to time to time
Even though we do not share the same mother
You are like a sister of mine

SISTER

Sister, we grew up side by side, playing childhood games
As we grew older we had more responsibilities and went through a
   change
One had to cook and clean
The other had to bathe and dress younger siblings
Sister we had good times and bad times too
But we sisters stuck like glue
Sure there were times we fought and scuffle, but we soon made up
And when others try to mess with us we did not take their stuff
Sister we are one of a kind we share the same blood
Sister, I shall love you until the end

COUSINS

Cousins, we play together when we were young
There were a bunch of us so we always had fun
Kids in the neighborhood would come and play
We were never bored we found things to do
First cousins, second cousins, third ones too
We share the same blood some from mom some from dad
Some are good, some are bad
Some are happy, some are sad
But we are family we share the same blood
We fought and mad up a time or two
No matter what we were there to see each other through
The good times and bad times too
We stuck close like ordinary families, do
We are children of related parents that makes us kin
We will love each other until the end

AUNTIE

The aunt who watched me through the Summer
Kept me with her children as though I did not belong to another
She made sure I was fed and with her children had fun
She made sure we were not bothered by no one
The auntie with a special smile and sweet heart
May are families never grow apart
We should cherish the memories when we were young
We should never forget were we came from

UNCLE

Uncle, the male who small nephews and nieces look up to
Uncle, you should always keep small change to give a time or two
Uncle, sometimes has to play a role of a father when their daddy is not
    around
So, uncle remember to be the man God wants you to be
Because every child likes to have a man they can look up to

NIECE

Niece, the child of my sister or brother
Niece, some aunts act like their mother
Niece, I hope you grow up to be a beautiful woman
Not only on the outside but within
Reach for your dreams
Aim high, never low
Remember in life there are many places to go

NEPHEW

Nephews are boys they are one of a kind
You can never tell what is on their mind
Always curious and getting into things
Yet they are the ones who carry on the family tree
So, nephew you stay strong and be the man God want you to be
Live life single and free
Because when you grow old you will have responsibilities

WHEN GRANDMOTHER BECOMES YOUR MOTHER

The age we live in is strange
Some mothers abandon their children and act derange
Some commit crimes and go to jail
Others get on drugs until their body gets frail
Some get to busy and just don't care
Their responsibilities they leave aside
Until their babies look to grandma and cry
Grandma has become a mother to her grand baby
Because their parents are out running the streets
Grandmothers love can be strong
Because they believe in nursing their own

GRANDMOTHER

Grandmother,
The woman who smiles graciously
When I look into her us I can see an older picture of my mother or me
Grandmother, the one who takes time to cook cake and pies
Grandmother, the one who get tissues and wipe the tears from your eyes
Our grandmothers are women we ought to love and respect
Because she took time out of busy schedule and time with you she spent
She owes no one any favors her children she raise
So if she spent time with you, you should behave
Cherish your grandmother so her love everyday
So your days can be long if your parent you obey

THE GRANDMOTHER WHO DESIRES TO STAY YOUNG

The grandmother who desires to stay young,
She doesn't have time to age she's too busy having fun
She wears clothes her granddaughter would not even put on
Her body swing like she is walking in a pond
A sixty-five-year-old woman acting like she's sixteen
Hopefully her children act matures,
Because if they follow in her footsteps
Who would be there for the children to adore

GRANDMOTHER

Grandmother,
A woman of virtue and honor
A mother due her respect and a nanny to her children's offspring
For thou age latch holds to her, her beauty still stands firm
As you look into the eyes the frail frames
A story of history you may see
One may be of pain, of broken dreams and years of struggles
The years of sacrifices for her family, if she was a teenage mother
The youngsters became her center attraction, growing up became
    immediately
Grandchildren she seen in her middle age, they call grandma like they
    are calling a page
Grandmothers of yesterday were the backbone for their descendants
She encouraged her babies and led them to the directions they went
Loving on her progenies, for she is our loving grandmother

REMEBERING GRANDMOTHER

IN MEMORY OF LOTTIE MAXWELL

Remembering grandmother, she was so sweet as she can be
When it came time to a get a whooping,
She'll tell you don't pick one switch but three
She would wake up in the morning
Cooking biscuits, rice, and sometimes steak too
When your around grandma eating you wish there was no other relatives
but you
She will send us out to pick berries or apples off the tree
So she can make a pie or a few turnovers too
When your around grandma, it seems like there's nothing she can't do
Living in the country where the water pump in front of the house
went dry
Thank God there was a spring near by
My brother had to fetch a few buckets of water several times a day
Because we not only had to drink it but had to use it to bathe
In a tin tub your body will squeeze
After three people if you were last, you will wish you could rinse
Having a grandma was fun, she would teach us
Make sure we did things right and made sure we did not fight
When she got weak, I was there to assist her
And by some things she need
For my loving grandmother had a house full of peace

GRANDFATHER

Grandfather bears an image of what my father may become
Will I follow in their footsteps when it is all said and done
That is why it is important to teach values to your sons
Morals to uphold the law and to respect everyone
Time is of the essence, society's values are low
Young men are walking around like there is no place to go
A man with strong leadership, need to be an example for them
Inspire them to press forward and conquer their dreams
And to seek God for their spiritual needs

GRANDPA

Some grandfathers want to stay youthful and swing with their sons
Have a young woman on his arms and his children's mothers are few
But there are some who looks forward to leaving an example for their
young
Living by godly standards a husband of one
Treating females with respect and influence his descendants to do the
same
Making their grandchildren know take life serious not to treat it as a
game
Teaching their males to be responsible for themselves and their family
Because you have to work for what you want in life nothing comes free

THE LEGACY OF A PRAYING GRANDFATHER

Grandfather grew up in church, a praying man was he
He passed it down to my father and my dad gave it to me
They believed in the power of God and teaching their children to live
    right
They realized living in this world our battle is not physical but a spiritual
    fight
They fought many wars on their bended knees
Praying for others that God will set free
They realize fatherhood was not limited to their own
But to all those that need a manly example to be shown
Thank God for the grandfathers who were fathers in deed
Passing down their legacy to their family tree

GRANDPA

(In memory of my grandfather Moses Yarbrough)

Grandfather kept plenty candy around
So when his grandchildren would come they would find
He kept some change too, because he might give someone a quarter
  or two
His words were few but he would smile, being around gramps would
  make time worth while
He had five children five girls and five boys
They were all grown when I was little, they no longer played with toys
A house full of cousins, uncles, and aunts too
Making sure the little ones do what they say do
Girly, he would call to the little ladies in the house
His home was like a mansion to me, three stores tall, high as a tree
Many would folk in his home, because there was plenty room to roam
Remembering his toothless mouth and fair brown skin
Make me realize how special it is to have grandfathers around

GRANDMAS, GRANDPAS, AND PEOPLE OF AGE

The was a time the youth respected their old
Took time to listen to the stories they told
They didn't take time to sassy them back, because they were afraid of
getting smacked
Grandpas, Grandmas, aunts, uncles, and friends too, they were all there
to encourage you
As time go on and their hair grows gray, strength turn to weakness
And their life begins to demise, one by one they begin to fade
O how I miss my grandparents, uncle, aunts, and people of age
Those who were pillars in my life are fading away
But still remember their laughs and knowledge
Things they could teach you things you would never learn in college
Wisdom of the age is very special, they taught you how to survive
without a hassle
As time go on and their memories I continue to contain
Soon someone would hold my picture in a frame

Poems of Different Situations

AFRAID

I won't be afraid no more
I will not let bad circumstances roar
I know I have God living within
So why should I hold down my chin
I won't be afraid no more
I will not let bad influences or doubt enter my mind
I will cast down all the strong hold that try to take over my life
Because I am riding God's ship and God controls the door

AFRAID 2

How shall I be afraid when God has my life
Is it because I don't believe His, Word
Do I only look for today and what this life has for me
Or do I look at the great beyond and see eternity
Do I dwell on life circumstances and get overwhelm with this earth
Or do I realize without God I can do nothing
And on God's strength rely

AFRAID 3

I am not afraid
Why should I be afraid
Why should I fear
When I know, I have a God who is near
Man can hurt the body, but God can destroy the soul
In Him I am complete and whole

AFRAID 4

Enclosed in a box, shutting out the world
Afraid of the future
Crippled by your past
You only behold life through a glass
Afraid of living, afraid to die
The fear you obtain bring tears to your eyes
And sometimes you look up into heaven and wonder why
God clothe the ravens, He put the moon and sun in the sky
Ask the Lord within your heart, so with you He can abide
Your past He will throw into a forgetful sea
In God you will have no sorrow
You spirit He will renew
Your fear God will take away
And you will rest in God and no longer be afraid

AN HONEST HUSTLER

They look around for a deal or away for money to make
They are an honest don't make that mistake
They may gather scattered cans to sell or find scrap metal thrown away
They are looking for an honest hustle to get an honest pay
They can be and adult or child too
There are a lot of people in this world trying to find something to do
Some have a job desiring to make extra money so there needs they can meet
Some are homeless beg for money to get food to eat
Some are children asking for change because a parent do not give
Times are hard jobs are few
People are looking for a honest hustle
No con, no games, nor looking for neighborhood fame
Just looking for honest hustle to live
So if you have any advice or a hand, please give

CHILDREN

Children are precious,
Innocent and sweet,
Children are what adults use to be
Children can be humorous, lovable, and kind.
Children sometimes help us to release worry from our minds
Children needs our attention, compassion and understanding
Children need our encouragement to move further in this life.
Children are mysterious and courageous
Children are what we make them.
Shall we surround them with love or hatred
Shall we show them the good in of this life or bad
Children,
Some are loved,
Some are hated,
Some are cradled,
Some are abandon,
Some are understood, and some misunderstood
Many children in many different situations
Many children with different faces
Some are sad, some are happy
Children are what we all should be in the sight of God
Not to rule, but easy to follow
Willing to learn and obey, everything our heavenly father say
God bless the children in this world today this is what I pray

CIRCUMSTANCES OF LIFE

The circumstances of life
Can drive you to do something right or draw you to do something wrong
A man who just lost his job
May not have money to pay his rent
Because on food all his money he has spent
Circumstances of life
Some things we can control and others we cannot
We have to take life one day at a time
Remember to keep God in front and not behind
God never told us life would be easy
But a cross we have to bear
He let us know every hair on our head is numbered and for us God do care
So while you face the circumstances of life do not let them get you down
Remember to rely on the power and strength of God for God will see
    you through

FOOD

Food
Comes in different styles and shapes
Food can be good tasting or bitter.
Steak, vegetables, candy, and cake, this is some of the things our natural body takes.
But we are made of a spiritual man too, he must eat the spiritual food.
Fasting and praying reading God's word
Eating of God's goodness
Taking time out to praise His holy name
Because without Him how would our spiritual man live.
That's the reason why we should thank Him for our natural and spiritual food
We can eat of them both, but it's up to each individual to chose
The natural food you can only eat while you're on earth
And after your living days are over, your body shall return to dust
Living spiritual is what God desires of us
Feeding your flesh and not your spirit, in hell you shall lift your eyes.
But eating right natural and spiritual in heaven eternally you shall feast

FRUSTRATION OF LIFE

The frustrations of life can get you down
Make you feel like there is no one else around
Make you feel like no one has troubles but you, but my friend that is not true
Everyone has things they have to face
One may worry if they have money to pay their rent
Another is not concern about the money he spent
One may be concern if she got food to eat
One person may not be able to pay their bills
While one has a lot of funds and he do not want to share with any one
He worries about the taxes he has to pay because he does not want to
    give them any way
One wants to stay single another desire a wife
This world can be full of misery and strife
The rich sometimes get distress because they have to deal with a lot of mess
The poor has their problems too, they have too many needs and the
    money is few
There are many frustrations in life
We need to be strong and face the things we need to go through
Ask God for guidance and wisdom too

A TINKLING LIFE

I was a giver, I truly was
I gave for praise not for love
I was the one who wanted to be seen
I kept a big smile, but inwardly I was mean
I wore my church clothes
I wanted the preacher to call my name
I was not Christ like, I did not show love
You could tell I was not a saint
Compassion you could not see
Neither would I bend on my knees
You see I am what you call a tinkling cymbal a sounding brass
I am like a wolf in sheep clothing
I wear a mask
I can be your father, your mother, your sister, your brother or you
Being saturated with the things of this world can turn your heart hard
God help those with false worship and call God's name in vain
May they wake up to see their worthlessness and God's Holy Spirit regain

INNER STRENGHT

Inner strength is what you need
When you don't have a shoulder to lean on
Inner strength is what tell you, you can
When others tell you, you can't
Inner strength is what you rely on when your heart is broken in two
Trouble is on every side and you don't know what to do
That is when you put your trust in God, because you cannot rely on yourself
Life on earth can sometimes make you feel like you're in hell
When all things fail that is when God steps in
If we abide in Him, Christ will be our inner strength

SUICIDE

Pressure is on every hand life is caving in
You feel like you have nowhere to turn
No hope or vision for the future you can see
No one you can turn to
To pour out your troubles to
So you feel fed up with life and everything is through for you
Life my friend may not be easy
Sometimes pain and heartache will come
But we must realize we cannot depend on ourselves
We got to rely on the Holy One
God is able to give you hope for tomorrow
Purpose for your life
Strength to fight oppositions
Dreams and vision for your future
When life for you feel like you are about to end
Turn to God and cash it in

A TREE

A tree grows tall and its roots goes deep
The branches are full of leaves or they lay on the ground beneath
We as saints need to be stable like a tree planted on earth
Not tossed with every wind or doctrine
But like a tree planted by the waters we shall not be moved
Everyone needs stability in their lives to be able to grow
If we ever want to be anything for God or in this life
We must realize we need to develop ourselves without envy and strife
So when you see a tree that has blossom growing in the wind
Don't let him have to ask you where have you been
For you will never grow fervent in Christ if you do not get stability in
    your life

WHY

Why do the justice system free some, and let others stay bound
Why is a question young children ask when they need something
  explained
Why is a question a cancer patient may ask, as they lay in pain
Why is a question a person frustrated with the circumstances of life
And their heart is full of strain
Why is a question we ask God when we are going through tribulation
We forget the Lord can deliver us from every situation
God said He would not put more on us than we can bear
So, if life cause you to question, why
Remember we have a Savior for you He died
Life will not always be easy as we live day by day
But we should recall God is our helper and He will strengthen us along
  the way

SERIES OF POEMS 1

Your flesh is whining
While your spirit is dining
With Jesus Christ new lining

Let your love show
While your eyes glow
Because Jesus love is pure as snow

Let the Lord lead you everyday
Let Him show you the rightful way
Whatever happens may be His will
Even though it affects your skills
Don't get mad or be upset
Just ask Him to lead you the way
Don't worry about the award He gives
Just let everyone knows that Jesus Christ lives
For we know, that there is a time to receive and a time to give
And now it is the time to let others know that Jesus Christ lives
There is a time to go through hell and a time to rejoice above
But whatever you do, do it in Jesus love.
Let Jesus lead you every way
He'll brighten every minute of your day

SERES OF POEMS 2

Let His love show wherever you go
Let His light shine
From your head to your toe
Let everyone know that Jesus Christ love glows
Anywhere
And any place,
Any time,
And any case,
Everyone,
And every race
Let Jesus Christ fill that empty space

God will help you anywhere
Any time, because He cares.
If you want the love He shares
Ask Him because my Lord cares

Help is always there
Because Jesus Christ really cares
If you really want the love He have
All you have to do is pray and ask
He'll welcome you with a big hug
Just ask Him in your heart
And He'll show you where to start
Just believe and He'll fill that empty heart

TIME

I wanted time to relax with me
But it just looked at a glance
I wanted time to rest my brow, and run my fingers through my hair
But it just laughed
I wanted time to sit in an easy chair, and kick up my feet
But it just walked away
I wanted time to ease my weary mind
But it said come back another day
For all of those people who do for everyone, and do little for themselves
For all those people who work endlessly and get a little rest for themselves
For all of those people who seek to meet the needs of others
And forsake the desire for themselves
Your moment on day will come

IM GOING TO RUN

I'm going to run, I'm going run that race of faith
I'm going to run, where God tell me to
And nobody will stop me from running my race
I'm going to run my race even though other people don't understand.
I'm going to run, my race holding God's big hands
I'm going to run, no matter who cross my pathway, because I'm going
  to follow the Lord
Now if someone cross my way and say, sit down girl you don't know
  day from day
I tell them don't worry, because God is leading my way
I'm going to run, even if someone calls me a devil,
Because they called my Savior the same thing too
I'm going to run my race until I hear the good Lord say, well done

PRAISE GOD WITH A CLEAN HEART

God said He want you to praise Him with a clean heart
No liar or backbiter, but with a clean heart
He is not impress with you fine jewels, wealth or your status
He wants you to have a clean heart
When you come to Jesus, you can't come with your nose in the air
Religious and self -righteous, you have to bow down before God with
    a clean heart
Come before the Lord with your all on the altar giving Him your all
    with a clean heart
He promised He will give you what you need and set your sin sick soul free

A PRAYER FOR NURSING STUDENTS GRADUATES

God we thank you for our journey
With perseverance and determination, we made it to the end
By the grace of God and His mercy
We conquered all our obstacles, circumstances and situations
We made it through the end
Now our nursing career we can begin
God be with us as we continue this journey of life
Guide us and shield us and watch over our families too
Help us to continue to acknowledge you in our lives
And cover us in your love

Amen

Poems of Death

THE NEW DAY

If someone close has passed away
Remember, it's a beginning of their new day
Don't get mad, cry, or pout
Just praise the Lord with a loud shout
Remember, their good times and their bad
But not feel sorry, feel glad
Because the ones who has left us
Is in Jesus good hands
So if you feel sorry for those who are deceased
Remember, now they're in great peace
If someone close has passed away
And you were too sad to start the day
I'm sure the deceased one would say
Let Jesus Christ lead the way

A REFLECTION AWAY

A picture on the wall
A gesture on your face
The memory of you is just a reflection away
The echo of your voice
Blowing in the breeze
The memory of you is just a reflection away
Your laughter, your tears
The moments we shared
You are just a reflection away
The conversations, the advice
Hold a key to my life
You are just a reflection away
It seems strange that you are gone
But the memory of you still lingers
So though your body is gone away
The memories of you is just a reflection away

DEATH TAKEN BY SURPRISE

Death can take us by surprise
Or it can give us a departing invitation
Some welcome it, while others try to turn it away
Death can be beautiful when you resting in the Lord
But it can be terrifying if you die without Christ
Why do some continue to play games like Russian roulette
They think they have their entire life to be saved, but time is running out
People die all the time they can be two years old to hundred and five
You need to choose to serve the Lord before death knocks at your door
Because if you accept Jesus in your life
You will live with Him forever

WHEN DEATH COMES

What do you do when someone suddenly pass away
How will you respond, how will you live
How will you face day to day
It may be your child, a loved one or friend
We wonder when will death end
Death has no limitations, of age, gender, race, color, or greed
No matter you position, death will come and how will you make your
transition
Make sure you are ready when death comes to your door
When your time comes you should welcome it and not live in horror
Death do not take a saint by surprise, there are times a believer can sense
their departure arrival
And others remain prepared, for we are told we know not the day nor
the hour our Lord should come
Some feel they may be alive to expect His coming, while others die in
the faith
Knowing the dead in Christ will arise first to meet our Lord in the air
What will you do when death comes

Poems of
Different Occasions
Written For Others Has
Been Slightly Rearrange
To Omit Names

=====

BEAUTY

Beauty is what we see we behold God's earth
We can see it in a flower as it blossoms beautifully radiant colors for us to see
We can hear sounds echoing through the air
Coming from birds, bees, cats, dogs, and all of God's creatures
Who can say whether or not they're rendering praise to their Creator
    on high
Now let us remember man the last of God's creation
For in His image we are created
For God is a holy God and every man should desire to be just l Him
By letting Jesus abide in our souls and then we're able to live free from sin

FAMILY

The love of family is precious
Like one like yours
With a husband for many years and children too
Honoring God and living a holy life
When circumstances arise it's good to know
You have an extended family too
The people of God, your church family is true
For grief over your loved one who pass away
Our prayer is God will strengthen you and brighten each day
May you continue to rely on the Lord
And I know the shoulder of your husband you can lean on
As a rose blossom in its season and flowers fade away
Our prayer is God continue to encourage your heart and brighten
    each day
As our Savior nourish your heart and His Word sooth your soul
He will continue to bless your family as His future for you all unfold

OUR WEDDING DAY

When I saw her I was mesmerize by her beauty
When I saw him, I saw a fortress someone to hold and protect me
As our friendship grew so did our love for each other
We decided never to depart but live our lives together forever
As a flower blossoms and release an aroma in the air
As a bird flies and ascends into the heavens
So shall our love flow as the water from the seas
May we let nothing come between our love
We shall seek guidance from God above
God bless the both of you and may your love continue to be true
For love can conquer anything you go through

WRITTEN FOR A GIRL WHO LOST HER FATHER

Daughter your father's baby girl,
I have seen the smile on your father's face
When your father let me know where I live my daughter is there
It may be hard for you knowing your dad is gone
This is why I wanted to say a few words to you in this poem
Always keep your head uplifted knowing your father really loved you
You were his little girl and is nothing too good for you
Hold the memories of your father close to your heart
Strive to complete your goals and finish your task when you start
My prayer is for God to look over you
And may you feel His love
And when you get your deepest low
Look to God above

WRITTEN FOR A SON WHO LOST HIS FATHER

What do you do when your hero you can no longer see
You ask God to help you face another day
Because He is the one who can give you strength to continue on your way
I watched the smile on your father's face as he spoke of you being in
    college
He was proud to know his son had a desire to attain more knowledge
For we know challenges will come ahead for you will be missing your dad
Hold on to your memories and that will help ease your pain
With your mother by your side and God up above
My prayer for you is that God surrounds you and let you feel his love

A MOTHER TO EVERYONE

A mother to her children
And to her nieces and nephews too
A mother to many people and not a few
A mother with love and understanding spreading concern wherever
    she go
To her foster children and extended family too
Without your motherly love what will your kin folk do
Keep your understanding and your wisdom too
Keep your long suffering and your peace
For possessing all these things make you unique
Thank you for your kindness and for lending a listening ear
To let me know you truly care
It is nice to know people like you are still around
Because you are like a treasure and a priceless jewel
May God continue to bless you and your family too
Because they are truly blessed to have a mother like you

THANKS FOR THE INTERVIEW

Time can go by fast
In a working day
People can approach you
In every sort of way
Do this do that a boss can demand
It is good to know for our lives God has a plan
I know your day is busy
As your clock out time approach
If your soul is weary you can ride upon God's heavenly coach
Thank you, for taking time out of your busy schedule to interview me

POEM FOR MOTHER WHO LOST HER SON

Like a sound of the beating of a drum
Echoing through the air in our mother land Africa
Like a willow blowing in the wind
Earth has open and claim life once again
A mother has lost her son
A sister has lost her brother
Like a sharp knife cutting deep the pain is felt
Can no longer hear his voice, nor touch his flesh
A picture you now hold a replica of the man you love and body embrace
Like the rhythm of the music racing the heart
Always hold on t your memories and never let them depart
There is not a song or word a person can say
As they watch their cold loved one lay
In time the pain will ease and grieve will go away
But as you dwell on the man that once was a child
Who is no longer here with you
Remember to keep your trust in God and he will bring you through

SO FAR AWAY

(Written for my mother)

Time has come, many days has past
And still your daughter is so far away
Months has vanished and a few years too
And still your daughter is so far away
Many things have happened and deaths has taken place
And still your daughter is so far away
Mother no matter the distance or few letters you may see
I always remember you on bended knee
Thou distance be between me and you
I will acknowledge God in your daily life
It's Him who will bring you through
I love you as my mother
And my mother you will always be
But serving God means a lot to me
So, mother keep a praying
Living a life bound to God and yet be free
Free from sin and worry
Because you would have turn everything over to God
And no matter what problems you face, He will be there with you
So mother I'm praying for you
I believe in God and I know what the Lord can do
No matter the distance between us, God is not so far away, so pray

SHOWING APPRECIATION TO AN EMPLOYER

For being a woman of love and concern
This I know because to me she have shown
She helped me find work when I was unemployed
I observed her to be a faithful mother and wife
One that volunteers her service and time to friends and organizations
As a former employee and friend
I pray that God will continually bless you and your family
I pray you all will continually grow in the knowledge of Jesus Christ
Hoping that you and you husband
Will continue to grow stronger as a man and wife
Until both of your beautiful children
Live to lead their own life
May all your days be long and full
May all your goals be achieved
As you all journey through this life

THE HEARTBEAT OF A MOTHER

(Written for a mother who lost her daughter)

A mother's heart is calm
When she knows her child is at peace and everything is well
A mother's heart races when she senses danger for her child
And causes her to be concern
A mother's heart can go into pieces when she loses one of her offspring
That she cherishes dearly
It takes the finger of God to bind that broken heart and sooth the pain
For the hurt can be excruciating and felt as the body returns to the body
 from the heart
As time goes on and you continue to heal
May your heart revive with memory of the daughter you love
May the thought of yesterday sooth your today and calm your tomorrow
Realizing you gave your child the best that you had
And now you must leave everything in God's hands
Because God understands the heartbeat of a mother

A COMMUNITY CENTER

(Written for a senior center)

To the community center
Staff, worker, participants and friends
You all care for my mother like she was family
You all act like an extended kin
For all the care and concern you all have shown
You all made my life easy as my mother's illnesses grown
Words cannot express the gratitude I feel for you all of you
I just want to say thank you for all you do
I know you all are a blessing to the families who need you all care
So you all be encourage as you all show your love and concern
And may God look down upon you all
And a blessing upon you all bestow
Keep showing the love for the needy
For a blessing you all will see
Because it is true you will reap what you have shown
Thanks is a small word and appreciate is too
But my prayer will continually go out to God for all of you
May God shine upon you all
For the blessing you all are to others

SURROGATE MOTHER

You bore a child too large for your womb to hold
When she came forth all of her burdens on you unfold
You had to deal with her attitude mood swings too
She had so much drama until you had to figure out what to do
You gave her tough love, the truth you did not withhold
You stood firm on your words, even thou she kept singing like a bird
It takes a special person to love someone who is difficult to love
I thank God for you, because you are like a gift from above
A surrogate mother, there is no one like you
To take upon a load, no one else could seem to hold on to
Maybe that child will realize a beautiful woman she can become
If she learns to listen to others and learn the meaning of humility
So, surrogate mother, I will like to thank you for all you do
Because there is not a woman as special as you

THE BIG BROTHER I LOST

(Written for woman who lost elder brother in memory of Doug)

You were the one I looked up to
You were my big brother
You were my best friend and there is no other
No one who can understand me like you
No one who can hold me like you do
I can't understand why you went away
I cry for you I my heart everyday
Asking God to help me with this pain
Because I need the Lord to help me to make it another day
I became angry with God, I had to ask Him a question
Why do the ones you love the most pass away
I don't know what God's answer will be, but one thing I want Him to do
Help me to deal with the pain in my heart
Help me to believe in you again
I don't think I can make it another day
I need you to help me, I need you to help me today

ME AND MY MATH

(Written for a college classmate)

Me and my math is not the best of friends
For when I try to catch hold to it, it seems to get away from me
I tried to leave it alone, but I need it, it doesn't need me
Why, I asked myself, will math be my best friend
I tried t grasp hold to it, but it slipped from my hands
Math, is over powering me, I gave in to that subject
Suddenly, a cry for help I made
Will someone help me fight, math this dominating thing
Well, a classmate became my friend and gave me a little advice
Math, is not so powerful, it is just a bunch of problems waiting to be
    solved
So remember when you are in class to get very involved
Making sure you pray before you enter the class
Ask the instructor for assistance when you need it
Remember to do your homework
Tell yourself you can do it
Holding on and never give up
Aiming to achieve the highest grade you can achieve
So classmate do the best you can and don't give up

A SOLEMAN PRAYER

(Written for a woman who had a miscarriage)

A solemn prayer, I must say today
Because something has just happened, that I cannot understand
My mind has become now weary from struggling through the
    disturbance around about me
For now, my Savior, I must seek
So shush, and please be quiet, let me have some peace
My present conversation is between Jesus and me
I don't need a telephone nor do I need to utter a word
For I must talk to God, and my prayer must not be unheard
So shush, and be quiet please as I say my solemn prayer
I must talk to God, for I know He cares
So please don't hand me a hanky a as the tears falls from my face
Just let them drop in their own place
For now, my soul is in grief and it doesn't really matter who sees
Because this solemn prayer is between Jesus and me
I don't need to hear a song nor a testimony
Just let everything be quiet, for now I need complete peace
For a solemn prayer I prayed today, and I'm waiting on my answer
And I know it's headed my way
Sister, we shall be silent as you go through your ordeal
But always remember when you need us, your spiritual family will be
    right there
So shush, we shall be quiet, and let you have your peace
We shall let you continue to pray your own solemn prayer
Cry if you must and also sob too
Because we are saying a solemn prayer just for you too

LOVE

(Newlyweds 1)

Love is what bring two together
Love is what someone shares with another
Love is when two marry and become one
My poem of love has just begun
There wedding day has arrived
Lord be with us I believe they prayed
Walk with us hand in hand
Let me be the woman and him be the man
Let us walk up right as we face the world together
Let us see you as we live each day
Believing you Lord, to guide our ways
Never let us forget your heavenly love
But let it flow continually from your fountain above
Love is what the newlyweds share
Bride continue to be virtuous, and achieve all your goals
Because one day, mother may be your role
Husband continue to keep groom very nice
After all, now you have a wife
Love is what brought you two to become one
And love is what will continually bring you all through, for God is love
Your special wedding day has arrived
Bless them Lord forever more

LOVE

(Newlyweds 2)

I waved my hand over the land
And claimed a husband for me would be
Then I opened my eyes and saw your face
Thinking to myself if I talk to him, I know a miracle would have taken
    place
I was told that a young lady admires me
Why me, I asked myself, but if it's true, please let it be
When we first had a conversation butterflies we felt
Not too long after, at the altar we knelt
Things did not come easy troubles began to arise
We thought we would never see eye to eye, so we decided to say farewell
    and good-by
We thought then everything would be roses, peaches, and cream
We cried out, Lord have mercy, what does marriage really mean
Though it wasn't easy and pressures pulled us apart
We had love for each other locked within our hearts
We found that marriage isn't easy, but we learned that it would be what
    we make it to be
We thank God for our trials, we thank God for His love
Because God has all power, whom power is from above
So look down upon us Father this we pray, bless our marriage each and
    every day
Help us to seek you more in this holy way
Aide us to cleave to one another, more as one and let nothing come
    between
Not family, nor friends, nor our ways
But let us become like you Father as we face each day
Lead us, guide us, watch over us we pray
Because with you Lord we plan to stay
Lord bless the newlyweds, today and tomorrow, in Jesus name we pray

LOVE

(Newlyweds 3)

A young woman full of compassion, understanding and life
Is this the reason your fiancé request for you to be his wife
I'm sure they both love the Lord
The groom loves to tarry before the Lord
The bride loves to sing and give God praise
They are both pulling together, taking their mind off of worldly things
Together they pull to be one, but soon dating will be over
And the happiness has only begun, sure, there may be heartaches
Time to pay bills, time of misunderstandings
And time that you may shed tears, but always remember this is a part of life
It's something one goes through, even husband and wife
So always remember no matter how hard trials get, that God will always
    be there
And the both of your needs will be met, so keep your head uplifted
As you walk down that aisle, knowing everything you went through
    was worth while
Love is beautiful when shared by two, especially the for the both of you
Wedding day will be over, and the both of you will look behind
    remembering good times
And yet pressing toward the future with God in the front
So, remember to stay encouraged, no matter what the problem may be
Through thick and thin, because what you go through the relationship
    will still be sweet
Days are getting closer, time is winning up
Time to pack all your stuff, your groom is waiting impatiently wringing
    his hands
Saying, Lord, when it's all over, I believe I will shout and go forth in a dance
So bride don't you worry time is soon to come for you and your groom
    to be one

A SPECIAL EMPLOYER

A special employer I work for
She is not a single lady neither is she a little girl
She's a mother and a wife
She has been a full grown woman half of her life
One day I was short of work, and to her I was introduce
And immediately she hired me without an excuse
She stopped teaching school to become a full time mother and wife
Her husband a full time lawyer
A son and a daughter, all of them as a family moves as one
She volunteers her time to others in need
She is thoughtful and considerate
She is a friend indeed
So special employer and family continue to live and keep yourself clean
Remember, I'm the one that clean your house
Never throw paper on the floor, neither throw it out the door
Never oh never if you every did
Because remember sometimes grown folks act like kids
But you can do it if you must
Because I'm just your housekeeper and I don't fuss
So continue to be a happy family
And remember to always stay sweet

STANDING IN CHRIST AS ONE

She is kind and very concern
He is a young man who stands firm
Both standing together seeking their heavenly Father's will
Arm in arm, hand in hand
Together with each other they decided to stand
In their love for God and one another
Standing, when times get hard, why, one may ask
Because they believe in God, standing, even if it means to forsake friends
Because God is the one their seeking t please and His friendship never ends
Standing on God's holy word believing and trusting in their Savior
    and Lord
The both of you keep and uplifted head,
Remembering God is yet alive, not dead
He's able to carry you both through
No matter what the task may be
Wife continue to play your music unto the Lord
Husband you continue to sing and do whatever God want you to
Never let what people say or think stop you
Just lift your head towards heaven and praise your Savior on high
Continue to stand together, continue to stand in Christ Jesus
And continue to let the love of God abide and shine in both of your lives
Because you both are setting for a good example of a sanctified husband
    and wife

I WILL BE WITH YOU FRIEND

Sometimes we wonder why things never go our way
And let times we feel like we can't face another day
But as time go by we realize where living by God's grace
So friend stay encouraged and keep an uplifted head
God's presence will always be there to carry you through each trail
He's a friend you can always call on, His number you can always dial
You can call Him in the morning
You can call God at noon
You can call Him at midnight hours
And you don't even need a dime
But remember whatever you ask of God
Let Him perform it in His time
God will always be a friend to you
And He wants you to know you're His too
So always be encouraged because in God you have a friend
And He will be there even to the end

A TRUE FRIEND

A true friend is hard to find
Someone you can talk to and unwind
A friend who can say a word or two
To encourage you to keep going through
So to a friend, I will like to say
Keep holding on because God is leading the way
Keep praying and seeking God for the salvation of your whole family
Never take down nor give in
For with Christ we will always win
Together we shall touch and agree
That the shackles on our loved ones will be loosen and they shall be set free
Thanks for all the encouragement, the rebuke, and advice
For you a godly woman truly is wise
Sister in Christ but a friend in deed
Remember God will supply all your needs
Just keep looking up to the master for in Him your strength lies
He is able to dry all the tears from your eyes
He will sooth every heart ache eases every pain
Because in Christ your strength you will regain

REMEMBERING THE LOVE OF MY LIFE

(Written for a woman who lost her mother)

You stroke my hair with your fingers
Your presence brightened my day
The knowledge you imparted to me lead me along the way
You raised your children with the love that only a mother could give
You taught us how to appreciate life and to the fullness live
You left us so sudden we did not have time to say good-bye
The only thing we can do right now is push the tears from our eyes
We wonder why you had to go away so quick
We wanted to tell you once again how we thank you for all the things
    you have done
But like a breeze of wind blowing in the air
We looked around and you were not there
To the family my prayers goes out to you
For we know it will take the strength of God to pull you through
For your mother's empty shell, you can only see
Because she has entered into her eternal sleep
Always cherish the memories of her smiling face and rely on God's
    amazing grace

FAITHFUL RECEPTIONIST

(Written for a junior college receptionist)

She greets every student with a smile
And makes you feel like going to college is worth while
She assists you in any way she can
Your pleasant countenance, your warm heart
Has ease the pathway of those who needed your guidance
Over the years I left and returned to the community college
I was able to update and regain knowledge
Your kindness and generosity has been true
I know when you leave your position
Your colleagues, you, they will be missing
Thank you for the faithful service you have shown
Now we have to release you on your own

AUTOMOBILE MECHANIC

(Written for school bus mechanic in Michigan)

I was driving down the road when my car broke down
I made a call to my mechanic, within a few minutes he drove around
He fixed my car several times, charging me a low price
It is not an easy job, to find an auto repair man that is nice
He takes the time to teach his sons the job, that he does best
At the garage he is a person you can count on
Mechanic, this is just a word of thanks, for helping me in the time of
    need
May you continue to be the kind of person that you are
Continue to be the caring father, that your children look up to
And I'm sure your wife is fond of you and love you too

MR DOORMAN

(Written for a night auditor co-worker)

Mr. Doorman, greets everyone with a smile
Mr. Doorman, makes sure everyone is ok and nothing is wrong
Mr. Doorman, is a gentleman and friendly too, he sometimes asks, what
    can I do for you
Mr. Doorman
Decided to retire from his job
Other opportunities he had to explore
So for himself he had to open the door
He had to leave behind past experience to pursue his dream
For those who are go getters and achievers we know what it mean
Just having a job is not enough
When vision and accomplishments are requesting you to fulfill
With yourself you play let's make a deal
I got to get rid of this, so I can do that
Like cards in your hand the deck you hold
Only you by the grace of God have power for your future to unfold
So as you take your quest for life
May your doors continue to open

Poems for Spiritual Workers and Leaders

A SOLDIER IN GODS ARMY

A soldier in God's army we all must be
We must fight this spiritual battle on bended knee
Our weapons are not carnal, like a knife or gun
But we win the spiritual battles by yielding to the Holy One
We must girt our loins with truth
Have on the breast plate of righteousness
Our feet must be shod with the preparation of the gospel of peace
We must wear our helmet of salvation and we must carry our sword
    which is the Word of God
We must take the shield of faith, so we be able to quench all the fiery
    darts of the wicked one
Be encourage when Satan comes to attack you
Remember you are a warrior and fight back
For we are able to preserver by prayer and supplication
For the Word tells us we should always watch and pray
We should seek the face of God every day
So we can be prepared for what comes our way
Remember if you wait on the Lord, your strength He will renew
Like an eagle you will mount on high, to a spiritual realm you will fly
You must realize you no longer live for you

CHILDRENS CHURCH LEADER

Children are the fruits of a woman's womb
Children are like plants in a garden needing to be prune
Some grow like wild flowers, because no one is there with them to attend
Some grow like weeds in a vacant field, not having love with in
Some are abandon, left to die
While some look up to heaven, to ask God why and cry
That is why it is important to have children's church leader like you
Someone who is concern, while others shun to give their time
Not realizing to neglect babies is a crime
All the time you take to give thought of all the things to do
To install love, joy, and hope to a little child who may feel blue
It takes a lot of dedication and a lot of time
Not a few pennies, nor nickels, or dimes
What we impart into our youth should be important to us
Our children are like precious jewels, there is not a price that we can pay
To make sure they live holy and take time to teach them that God is
    the way
So, leader stay encourage and keep carrying the vision for every child
Because your labor is not taken for granted and God will surely repay
So keep your head uplifted and the prize before your eyes
Because you are truly one of God's holy child

A LEADER FOR THE CHILDREN

One, two, three, where will children be if there is no one responsible for me
Four, five, six, who shall I pick who will be willing with the kids to assist
Some are too busy, some run out of time
Some would rather sit in church service and recline
Faithful workers with children who are dedicated are hard to find
But thank God for you someone who is always on their job
One who walks in their godly authority and the children know they are
    the boss
No jumping, no screaming, you over there, sit down
It is time to study God's Word not to clown
She gives the children the message loud and clear
The children listen to their leader because they know they care
Being dedicated t children is not an easy task
But it is something God requires of us and ourselves a question we
    should ask
Are we teaching our children by precepts and by being an example
Are do we neglect to say there is a heaven and a hell
Do we tell them life is just a gamble
My friend we have a responsibility to impart life to every child
They are the future in the kingdom and in Christ we want them to abide
So, leader stay encouraged and keep doing the will of God
For his yolk is easy and his burden is light

GOLDEN YEARS

(Written for a presiding bishop)

I went through many trials as I traveled through this land
Me and my wife walking hand in hand as we followed God's command
We have friends and family to forsake us
As we were doing what God had us to do
No one really knew the troubles we shared
No one really knew the burdens we bear, but we know God really cares
We've been lied on, miss treated, often misunderstood
But we didn't let that defeat us we kept doing God's will
I have traveled many years on this holy highway
There were times I left my wife alone to fall on her knees and pray
See, I had to get alone in my secret closet to talk with God along the way
Walking this road sometimes can be easy, but sometimes it gets very
    hard
I prayed, Lord, lead me and never forsake me, as I travel day today
Because there are times I'm just not able to see my way
For, truly, I had to walk the walk of faith, I relied on my Master every
    single day
Through these years of toil, I've gained patience, to deal with almost
    every situation
I've gained hope which gave me a stronger determination
I've gained longsuffering to deal with every contrary spirit
I've gained peace, peace within and among my brethren
I've gained joy which gave me laughter even when things got tough
I've gained many things along this road some has been revealed and
    others remain untold
But there is one gaining that sticks out most of all and that is love for
    my friend
Love for my brethren, family too, but most of all my love God
See, family, brethren, and friends, I must continue to hold my Master's
    hand

Even though my body has aged, and my hair is turning gray
I must still listen to what my heavenly Father says
He is the one that has kept me, even when I was young
Now I know there is one that kept me and God is the One
For, I have been like gold tired in the fire, through my years of travel
　　with God along this way
So now, I've have reached my golden years
I've waited so long for this day, but I must continue my journey
I must continue to fight the fight of faith
For, the race is not given to the swift, nor the strong, but to him that
　　endure this holy way
I shall continue not by my power, nor by my might, but by my God's
　　Spirit
For this is the only way
For God has everything I need and through Him I shall succeed
So, I must continue to run this race, until my course is over
For, when I have finish my fight of faith
I want to here my Lord, Master, and Savior say to me well done

O SWEET MOTHER

(Written for pastor's wife)

O sweet mother who we love so dearly,
She labors with us not just daily but yearly
Her smile is pleasant as she shows us that she is concern
Her actions of love speak, a lot louder than words
She speaks with authority as she chastises her children
She is our spiritual mother, and we lover her very dearly
She encourages her children to progress in life
She is none other than, our pastor's wife
She hoofers over us like a hen does her biddy
She is very free hearted with us, she's not nitty
O mother of our people we love you very much
Because you seem to brighten up, everything you touch
O momma may seem fussy as she tries to get us to do what we ought to do
But she doesn't do it to be bossy, she does it because she cares for us
So let us lift up our spiritual mother and encourage her as much as we can
Spiritual mother, keep holding on to God's hand

ANOTHER PRAYER AWAY

(Written for pastor and wife)

My dear brother and my sister, whom I love very dearly
Whom I usually write occasionally, not just yearly
When you do not receive a letter which you can see
One was written for you but it was between Jesus and me
For when I get too busy to write with my hands
In my spirit from the table of my heart I begin to write unseen
Lord look over my brother and sister, strengthen from the letter that is
    invisible
Speak encouraging words when they need to hear it
Open doors and meet their every need
For I often write letters to Jesus because He is a speedy postman
Who delivers messages better than any delivery man
His memorandum arrives just on time, it's called the prayer line
So when you don't see a letter it's not that I'm not concern
But I just tapped into an invisible system God's heavenly throne
So both of you always be encourage and keep an uplifted head
Remember God is always present for you,
The Lord will see you through

OUR ASSISTANT PASTOR

Our assistant pastor
She believes in praising the Lord
She stands up for God she is not shame
She stands beside her pastor
Encouraging him along this righteous way
Knowing divided we shall fall, but together we will stand
She's not only a hearer, but a doer of God's Word
She is compassionate, kind, and sweet
Her faith is in God, because in Him she is complete
Always keep an uplifted head while you walk this narrow way
Keep being faithful in your works and deeds
Always remembering God will take care of your needs
Keep standing behind your pastor encouraging him along this
    tedious way
Realizing that you are his other shoulder in the gospel in this last and
    evil day
Keep your mind uplifted, above the problems in your life
Keep walking forward to that eternal light
Keep watching, praying and fasting
Keep reading and preaching God's Holy Word
God is a hearer of all prayers and yours voice is not unheard
You are His chosen child and He loves you very much
You are the apple of God's eye, because in His will you abide
So assistant pastor be encouraged
As you walk this straight and narrow way
And as you walk always remember
God will be with you each and everyday

THE WORD

God spoke the Word which brought everything into existence
The Word became flesh and dwelt among us
He lived a life free from sin
He showed compassion is his way
He healed the sick and raised the dead
He died on the cross and gave up the Spirit
That we may partake of Him by letting His Spirit abide within
So be encourage as you walk this narrow way
Knowing that Christ has walked before you and the way has been made
    straight
He said all our sorrows and grief he would bear
Because for us he cares
Thy days may get dreary, and dark hours may come
Turn to Jesus, because He's the One
He's the one you can always turn to
He's the one who will brighten up your days
He will always answer your prayers, just believe Him when you pray
Turn everything into His hands
God is willing, and able and most of all He cares
He can do that which seems impossible for you
So don't forget the Lord is everlasting
He'll bring you through
So keep your head uplifted
Continue to preach the Word of God
Continue to play your music skillfully
Because the gift you are using is not your own, but to be used to glorify
    God in the highest

OUR PASTOR ANNIVERSARY

(Written for a pastor in Montgomery AL)

Our Pastor's Anniversary
It only comes once a year
When that day arrive, we ought to thank him with a cheer
Hurrah for our pastor, one of God's faithful warrior
One of God's faithful warriors', one who deserve this cheer
Why, one may ask, why cheer this man today
After all he's just a man God create
Why, replied one of the cheerers, that said hurrah very loud
Because there were many days he cried on his knees
For many of his sheep's that could not spiritual see
He took food from his table to feed someone else in need
He sacrificed and gave what was his
At times he went lacking doing for his wife and kids
He even went calling on sick saints at late midnight hours
Praying the prayer of faith because he knew that God had all power, he
     gave sound advice
Married those who decided to take a wife
He watched some of his sheep go astray
But that didn't stop him because he knows how to pray
He went to God for himself, he didn't accept, hear say
He preached the Word of God no matter what the cost
Because he loves God his master and his Boss
He didn't take down for the worlds way, but he cried loud and spare not
     holiness is the way
God seen that he could be used, as a warrior and a leader in his army,
     a firm man
Let's thank God for our leader, hurrah, hurrah, hurrah
Haven't you read I Timothy 5:17, a man of God is worthy of double honor
I thank you Lord, thank you Lord for this man of God
If that is not enough my friend, read I Timothy 6:1-2

Then you'll understand not thanking God for your pastor is not a wise
    thing to do
If God says he is worthy, then who are you
One other person we will remember
His wife who stick with him through thick and thin, from the beginning
    to the end
When others said he would lose, she said he would win
She is the sweetest cheerleader of us all
She is there to prop him up when everything seems to be going rough
My friend why do you think pastor's wives are mean
And say all they want to do is spend a lot of green
Don't you know they give a lot of which they receive
It was God that blessed them to prosper, because in Him they believed
Many things they went through, that others did not see
My friend he's a man of God just let him be
For we are not to touch God's anointed and do His prophet no harm
We're going to thank God for them, by letting them rest in a honored seat
Giving them a token t show our love will be sweet
Being rewarded from God above will make it more complete
Happy Anniversary to our Pastor and his wife
We pray you both say encouraged in this righteous way
Knowing God is always there to lead the way

UNNOTICE LABOR

The type of labor, people try to avoid
The type of labor, which never seem to be applaud
The type of labor free of color and fashion too
The type of labor, no one knows but God and you
No one knows the sacrifice you take as you prepare the food you make
The countless hours going to the grocery store
Thinking you have purchased enough and need to return for more
The time you spent planning the meals, hoping that the saints you feed
    are fulfilled
Missing service to make sure everyone is served, truly a gold metal you
    deserve
People like you possess a certain character that others cannot contain
Serving thinking of the need of others rather than your own
Some think serving is degrading, not realizing the one that serve is great
    In, the eye sight of God
Your spirit of humility, compassion, and love goes far
Your spirit illuminates the ones who come into your presence
As one who admires your spirit of servitude
You truly are a virtuous woman

FOLLOWING YOUR EXAMPLE

As Naomi was to Ruth, that is how you behold your elder woman
With love and respect, you follow their rule
How precious it is for a woman of youth to receive impartation from a
    mature woman of God
If only a young maiden can understand how much their life can be
    enriched
Their life can be to have a godly mother to hold their hand
Sister this is what I see in you as you labor with your mentors
Willing to serve with a smile and with a sincere heart
No matter what your trial may be from God do not depart
Continue to be humble and continue to learn from your piers
For those with a meek heart God will hear
He knows the desires of your heart and your every need
God is the one who can make you complete and your goals He will help
    you to succeed
So keep your head uplifted and your eyes focus on the Holy One
For He can only say servant well done

LABOURS TOGETHER

God's Word let us know we are laborers together with God
Sometimes when believers come together everyone wants to be boss
But it is beautiful to see, the saints work together in unity
Everyone looking out for one another and the agape love is shown
This is what I see in you as you sacrifice and serve
A gold metal you truly deserve
It is easy for some to serve when in a camera they are in view
But those who labor when they are not seen are few
God knows the ones who serve Him from the heart
Those are the ones, from God they will not depart
So keep your head up high and continue t do what God want you to do
Remember you can only give an account for what you do
God is able to carry you through any situation, any trial, and any
    temptation
All you have to do is keep trusting His Word

Song Lyrics

FEELING FREE

Me a child whose young

I have no fun, I have no fun

I spend my time in fields working hard to get a meal.

Then, I cry with pain my heart given me strain, but then God gave me laughter feeling free.

Verse 2

For man can only hurt the body that I have, but the Lord can hurt my soul. I have a feeling of being free, so free in my heart I shall be. Feeling free (3x), then God gave me laughter, feeling free.

Verse 3

My heart might have pain, my feet locked with chains, but still I have a feeling, feeling free. Feeling free (3x) then God gave me laughter feeling free.

YOU ARE THE GOD OF MY TRANSITION

Verse 1
You ae the God of my transition bringing change in my life
Taking me through all my opposition that I face everyday
This is my prayer I pray as I go through my change
Let me be the vessel you want me to be and yield fruit of righteousness
Verse 2
You are the God of my transitions bringing change in my life
Taking me through all my circumstances that was brought my way
This is my prayer I pray that in my life you will have your way
And all I've been through, I want to still give glory to you because my
    life you have changed
Verse 3
You are the God of my transition bringing change in my life
As I go through my change facing disappointment, hurt and pain
I will continue to give you the praise because you are the only one that
    can bring me through
Verse 4
You are the God of my transition bringing change in my life
Just continue molding me into what you want me to be
Because one day I want to lay at your feet

IF YOU ARE DISCOURAGE YOU CAN BE ENCOURAGE BY THE LORD

Verse 1

When problems come and get you down and you don't have no one to talk to.

Just fall down on your knees and begin to pray, for the Lord listen to every word you say.

All you have to do is pray. (chorus)

Verse 2

When you are not able to reach goals in your life and everything you try to accomplish fails for you. It makes you burden down in despair, until you feel like no one cares. Just pick up your Bible and begin to read God's Word and let His Word comfort you because whatever God got prepared for your life. That's why I say... (Chorus)

Verse 3

There's not a friend like Jesus, not one. There's no on that can be with you, like the Lord can. He sticks by your side through thick and thin, and He will help you to the end. That's why I say... (chorus)

Chorus

If you are discouraged you can be encouraged by the Lord (4x)

LORD WE WORSHIP YOU

Sopranos, Altos, Tenors: Lord we worship, we worship you, we worship you (twice)
Choir: Yes
Tenor: Thou art our mighty Counselor
Altos: Thou art our prince of peace
Sopranos: Thou art our great deliverer. That is why we worship
Altos: That is why we worship
Tenor: That is why we worship
Choir: You

Soprano: Lord we worship you
Altos: we worship you > (repeat sequence twice)
Tenors: we worship you
Choir: That is why we praise your holy name
Altos: Because without you we are nothing
Tenor: Nothing
Sopranos: Nothing. Lord, we worship you
Altos: We worship you
Sopranos: Nothing. Lord we worship you
Altos: We worship
Tenors: We worship you
Choir: Thou art our great Warrior mighty in battle, mighty in strength (twice)
Without you Lord we're not able to fight in this spiritual battle, in this spiritual fight.
Tenors: That is why
Altos: That is why
Sopranos: That is why
Choir: We worship

LIFE BEYOND THE CLOUDS

Life may not be easy as we face it every day, we look into our life and it seems like a picture of a cloudy day. But we got to remember God goes farther than the clouds, we have to look through the clouds and see a brighter day.

(chorus)

Verse 2

Sometimes situations and circumstances too, seem to weigh you down and put you in despair. So fly like an eagle and excel above this world, look unto the sky and fly, fly.

(chorus)

Verse 3

God our heavenly Father knows what we go through, we got to put our trust in Him and know He'll bring us through. For we got to realize this world is not our home. For our home is beyond the clouds.

(chorus)

Chorus

There is life beyond the clouds you have to look into the horizon and see the bright sunshine, (twice)

See God cares for you and he'll bring you safely through, for there's life beyond the clouds

IM BELIEVING GOD FOR YOU

I'm believing God for you
I'm believing for the impossible
I'm believing Him to do the things that man said it could not be done

I'm believing God for you
I'm believing for the impossible
I shall hold on and I shall not doubt, because without faith there is no
way out

I'm believing God for you
I'm believing for the impossible

PLEASE LORD HEAR US WHEN WE PRAY

Please Lord hear us when we pray
Choir: Pra-ay. For we need you to make it, through this world.
Soprano: We cannot make it
Choir: Through this land without you
Tenor: When trails comes to Choir: Buff us
Tenor: We'll know you'll be right Choir: There
Soprano: Lord, we need your strength
Choir: To make it through this land
Soprano: Please, lead us
Choir: Each day. For we need you to make the way
Tenor: Trouble is all Choir: Around
Tenor: Sickness is through
Choir: The land. If anyone can help we know you can
Soprano: Please send forth Tenor: Your mighty
Choir: Deliverance. Please hear your people as we pray
Tenor: We come humble as we
Choir: Know how Tenor: On our knees we do
Choir: Bow. Lord, please hear us when we pray. (twice with altos)
Altos: Lord Jesus (twice with choir)
Choir: Come. For we need you to make it through this land
Tenor: Please receive our prayer (5x with choir)
Choir: Prayer (5x)
Soprano: Lord we
Tenor: Need
Choir: You. To make it through this land. Please hear our prayer

TOGETHER ME AND MY LORD SHALL BE

Together me and my Lord shall be throughout eternally
I shall dwell in His home
For I love Him and need Him, and think lots of Him for He is my one
and only love
Verse 2
Together me and my Lord shall be throughout eternally
For He is my Savior and my Lord
For He said in my Father's house there are many mansions
And you shall be with me in my home
Verse 3
Together you and your Lord can be throughout eternally
For He loves and cares for you
All you got to do is let Him in your heart
And let Him live inside of you
For He promises never to leave, nor forsake you
Together you can live with God eternally
(Repeat verse one)

VICTORY SONG

Soprano: Victory
Altos: Victory
Tenors: Victory
Choir: Victory (all twice)
Choir: God has given us (3x), victory
We have victory over sin, we got victory over our problems. God had given us (3x) victory.

Sopranos: Victory
Altos: Victory > (twice)
Tenors: Victory
Choir: Victory
Choir: God has given us (3x) victory. We have victory over trials, we have victory over tribulations. God has given us (3x) victory

Altos: If you want the victory claim it
Sopranos: Claim the victory
Tenors: I got the victory
Choir: Victory, victory, oh victory (3x)
Sopranos & altos: Victory in Jesus, victory in Jesus
Tenors: I got the victory (twice)
Choir: Victory

NO YOU CANT TURN US AWAY

No, you can't drive us away (twice).
God said suffer little children to come unto me.
You can't turn us away.

No, you can't drive us away (twice).
We are descendants of Abraham you got to teach us what God command.
You can't turn us away.

No, you can't drive us away (twice)
God said if you don't come as a little child you can't enter in.
You can't turn us away.

No, you can't drive us away (twice).
God said out of the mouth of babes come perfected praise.
No, you can turn us away.

Thank you Jesus, thank you Lord (twice)
You didn't turn us away
Hallelujah, thank you Lord (twice)
You didn't turn us away.

WARRIORS THEME SONG

We are warriors in God's army yes we are (twice)
We will fight this spiritual battle; we will fight until we die
We are warriors in God's army yes we are.
We will lift the standard of holiness yes we will (twice)
We will let the light of Jesus shine in our lives
We are warriors in God's army, yes we are
God is our keeper, God is our guide, in our hearts we will let Him abide
We are warriors in God's army, yes we are (twice)
Satan has been defeated, by our God. Under our feet upon the devil we
    shall trod
We shall lift this holy banner throughout eternity
We are warriors in God's army, yes we are (twice)
Come and follow us as we follow Christ, then, you will be a witness of
    this holy life.
We are new creatures in Jesus Christ, we are the same and this place is
    not our home.
We are just pilgrims traveling through this land
We are on are way to heaven to see our sacrificed Lamb.
We will fight this spiritual battle (5 times)
We are warriors in God's army, yes we are. (twice)
God is Commanding Officer; He is the greatest warrior of us all
We are warriors in God's army, yes we are

WE WORSHIP YO TODAY

We are the children of Abraham
We walked through the Red Sea on dry land.
And we worship you today, today and we worship you today

We survived the attack of the enemy. We were captives but you set us free.
And we worship you today, today, and we worship you to

Our souls were lost we went astray, you died on the cross our debt you paid
And we worship you today, today and we worship you today
For you saved our soul and made us whole.
And we worship you today, today and we worship you today

YOUTH OFFERING SONG

We're not going to be stingy, no.
We're going to give (3x) (twice)
We're going to give God some of our money, we're going to give God
some of our money, we're going to give God some of our time, we're
going to give God our whole heart
We're going to give (3x)
You can't beat God giving, no.
You need to give (3x)
You need to give God some of your money, you need to give God some
of your time. You need to give God your whole heart.
You need to give (3x)

Printed in the United States
By Bookmasters